ANOTHER
101 QUIRKY
& CRAZY
PHRASES & SAYINGS

What They Mean
&
Where They Came From

MICHAEL SCHLUETER

ANOTHER

101 QUIRKY & CRAZY PHRASES & SAYINGS

Michael Schlueter
Copyright 2019 Michael Schlueter

ISBN 978-1-79342-755-7

Dedication

For Mom and Dad. Your love, support and guidance taught me how to aspire to a higher ideal.

ANOTHER
101 QUIRKY & CRAZY PHRASES & SAYINGS

You probably hear or say them every day - those quirky little sayings that seem to perfectly describe or solve a particular situation. I had so much fun writing the first 101 Quirky Phrases book, that this sequel was bound to happen! I must admit, it's turned into a bit of an addiction for me! I'm hooked and I believe you will be too!

So, here's a brand-new collection of all-time favorites like; "We'll Cross That Bridge When We Come to It," and, "Led on a Wild Goose Chase." They sound so matter-of-factly and downright smart when we say or hear them. But honestly, I never really knew what most of them meant and for sure didn't know where they came from - and most people I know didn't either. So, here's the new collection of some I'm sure you're familiar with, complete with their meanings and sometimes very quirky, and perhaps debatable origins. Pass it around at your next family gathering or office party and share some laughs!

I hope you enjoy!

Michael

CONTENTS

CONTENTS

CONTENTS

CONTENTS

"LONG STORY SHORT"

Meaning

To give a short version or only the conclusion of a long-winded narration or story without any extra details.

Origin

The idea of abbreviating a lengthy story is ancient, however, this precise expression has been used since the 1800s. American poet and naturalist Henry David Thoreau played on it in a letter in 1857; "Not that the story need to be long, but it will take a long time to make it short."

"YOU BET YOUR BOTTOM DOLLAR"

Meaning

Usually said when someone is absolutely certain that something will occur.

Origin

This saying has its origins in card playing. When a card player would place their bet, they would pull money off the top of the stack of money they had in front of them. To "Bet Your Bottom Dollar", meant they were betting the bottom dollar and all the others on top of that.

"ACE IN THE HOLE"

Meaning

A hidden advantage or resource that is kept in reserve until needed.

Origin

This comes from the game of poker, where a card dealt face down and kept hidden is called a 'hole card', the most advantageous card being the ace.

"WHAT GOES AROUND COMES AROUND"

Meaning

The basic understanding of how 'karma', the law of cause and effect work. Simply meaning, 'you get what you give'.

Origin

The earliest use of this phrase in print is in 1974 in a book by Eddie Stone. However, the idea on which this phrase is based goes back centuries and is in the Bible, 'as you sow, you shall reap'.

"WE'LL CROSS THAT BRIDGE WHEN WE COME TO IT"

Meaning

To deal with a situation only if and when it occurs, not to worry about it until it actually happens.

Origin

The earliest recorded use of this is in Henry Wadsworth Longfellow's poem written in 1851, "The Golden Legend", the story of Christianity during the Middle Ages.

"SOMETHING'S ROTTEN IN DENMARK"

Meaning

Things are unsatisfactory, there is something wrong.

Origin

This originates from Marcellus, a guard, talking to his philosophical comrade, Horatio in Shakespeare's play, Hamlet, Act 1, Scene 4, and refers to the rotten, corrupt political situation Denmark is facing.

"KEEP ON TRUCKIN"

Meaning

An encouraging mindset that people should stay true to themselves and not let other people or circumstances get them down.

Origin

In 1968, American underground artist Robert Crumb designed the comic character of a man drawn in Crumb's distinctive style, strutting confidently across various landscapes. His iconic image and the phrase became wildly popular during the 1960s and 70s by young people of that generation.

"THE EARLY BIRD GETS THE WORM"

Meaning

This is a very old proverb that emphasizes the importance of starting something early on to maximize the potential outcome and achieve the most success.

Origin

This English expression was first recorded in John Ray's, A Collection of English Proverbs in 1670: 'The early bird catcheth the worm.'

"GOD WILLING AND THE CREEK DON'T RISE"

Meaning

A whimsical way of saying that a person will successfully carry out some task provided that no unseen obstacles are put in their path.

Origin

Earliest written records of this saying date around the middle of the nineteenth century and is believed to be referring to the difficulty of travelling on dirt roads that forded rivers and streams, where a sudden storm and rising water would render the route impassable.

"NO GOOD DEED GOES UNPUNISHED"

Meaning

The idea that kind, beneficial actions often go unappreciated and sometimes are even met with outright hostility.

Origin

This originated as a bit of a comical take on the moral philosophy, 'No evil deed goes unpunished; therefore, no good deed is unrewarded.' This phrase has often been attributed to playwrights, Clare Booth Luce, Oscar Wilde, and journalist Walter Winchell, among others.

"GO BIG OR GO HOME"

Meaning

An expression and attitude that encourages someone to be extravagant, to go all the way, and to do and experience something to the fullest extent possible.

Origin

Said to have originated in the 1990s as a sales slogan for oversized Harley Davidson pipes. However, some claim this American idiom originated in the sports of mogul snow skiing and surfing, where participants taunted each other to 'Go Big or Go Home'.

"NO SHIT SHERLOCK"

Meaning

A sarcastic response thanking someone as "Sherlock", as if they just solved some mystery or answered a tough question that everyone already knew the obvious answer to.

Origin

This phrase became very popular in America in the 1940s and 50s and is still widely used today.

One of the earliest uses of this phrase in the movies was in the 1986 blockbuster film, 'Little Shop of Horrors', where Audrey II, the strange and interesting plant, says this to Seymour, played by actor Rick Moranis.

"FIRE IN THE HOLE"

Meaning

A warning that is usually shouted meaning to 'watch out' as something bad is about to happen.

Origin

This originated in the American coal mines where miners used dynamite to loosen rock. Miners used this warning to alert fellow workers to take cover. In fact, mining regulations required the warning to be verbalized three times before ignition.

"IT'S COLDER THAN A WELL DIGGERS ASS"

Meaning

Old slang, used in cold weather to place emphasis on how extremely cold it is.

Origin

This is a reference to the old days of well diggers when they would dig the well by hand and had to be fairly deep in the ground. As they dug, their ass would be against the side of the hole which was always cold and damp.

"IF IT SOUNDS TOO GOOD TO BE TRUE, IT PROBABLY IS"

Meaning

A caution to be suspicious of something that appears to be much better than normal or that you expected.

Origin

Various forms of this phrase date back to the 16th century and were used to describe many different situations, one of the most popular of which always involved financial opportunities and money schemes.

"NOW YOU'VE OPENED A CAN OF WORMS"

Meaning

Metaphorically speaking, to open a can of worms is to examine or attempt to solve some problem, only to inadvertently complicate it and create even more trouble.

Origin

Originating in the United States in the early 1900s, it referred to the metal cans that earthworms were sold in by fishing bait stores. If the lid was inadvertently left off the can once opened, the worms could wriggle out and escape. So, once you've opened a can of worms you could have a problem on your hands.

"RIDING THE GRAVY TRAIN"

Meaning

A position or situation where a person or group receives excessive and sometimes unjustified money or advantages with little or no effort on their part.

Origin

This phrase originated with American railroad workers of the 1920s and referred to the easy work but high paying runs they sometimes were on.

The rock music group Pink Floyd referenced record companies and their execs in their song, 'Have a Cigar' as 'riding the gravy train' on the backs of the musicians.

"THE BUCK STOPS HERE"

Meaning

Responsibility is not passed on beyond this point. It stops here.

Origin

A sign with this inscription was on the desk of retired US Army Colonel A.B. Warfield in 1931 but the phrase was passed along to President Harry S. Truman as a gift in the form of a sign for the President's desk by his friend US Marshall Fred M. Canfil and Truman popularized it with his Missouri plain-speaking attitude.

"A GLUTTON FOR PUNISHMENT"

Meaning

Someone who habitually and eagerly takes on burdensome or unpleasant tasks or unreasonable amounts of work.

Origin

Originating in the late 1800s, this English idiom is based on the literal meaning of the word 'glutton', referring to someone who will eat or drink until their belly aches, causing them to feel miserable and punished.

"BADA-BING BADA-BOOM"

Meaning

An expression that implies that a task or activity was easy to complete and accomplish – 'just like that' - Presto!

Origin

This Italian-American phrase is believed to have originated from Italian tenors at the New York Metropolitan Opera during the reign of the late Rudolph Bing. When Mr. Bing did something they didn't like, the would mumble, "itsa badabing." The "badaboom" came when they were fired for daring to criticize him.

It also gained popularity after being used in the first Godfather movie, when Sonny (James Caan) says it to Michael (Al Pacino) referring to 'whacking' some of their enemies.

"YOU'RE EITHER BUSY LIVING OR BUSY DYING"

Meaning

This refers to the power of a person's mindset and positive thinking. Circumstances in life only become insurmountable if allowed to invade and take control of one's mind.

Origin

This saying became very popular after it was used in the 1994 classic movie, 'Shawshank Redemption' when Andy Dufresne, played by Tim Robbins, said to his fellow inmate Red, played by Morgan Freeman, "Life comes down to a simple choice: You're either busy living or busy dying."

"PRACTICE WHAT YOU PREACH"

Meaning

Usually used in reference to someone whose behavior is in direct contradiction to the way they speak and tell others to act and behave.

Origin

Like many sayings, this one comes from the Bible, in Matthew 23:3 and reads; "So you must obey them and do everything they tell you. But do not do what they do, for they do not practice what they preach.

"IT WAS DEJA' VU ALL OVER AGAIN"

Meaning

A feeling of having already experienced the present situation.

Origin

This quote is attributed to New York Yankees catcher Yogi Berra in 1951 when Ted Williams of the Boston Red Sox popped up a foul ball that should have ended the game and ensured a no-hitter for pitcher Allie Reynolds. But Yogi dropped the ball, giving Williams another chance. Unbelievably, on the next pitch Williams pops up a foul ball identical to the first, but this time Yogi makes the catch and ensures the no-hitter for Reynolds. It was "Deja' vu all over again!" said Yogi.

"DON'T HOLD YOUR BREATH"

Meaning

Something said cynically to suggest that what has just been mentioned is unlikely to happen any time soon, if at all.

Origin

This expression dates to the mid-20th century American English. A related expression is to wait "with bated breath" which dates back to Shakespeare in the 16th century. Holding your breath is a natural reaction to an anxiety provoking or stressful situation. "Don't hold your breath" assumes that the person being addressed will, in fact, hold their breath in anticipation.

"WHO YA GONNA CALL"

Meaning

Often used in situations where something has gone wrong and someone needs to deal with it.

Origin

Made famous by musician Ray Parker Jr's theme song for the 1984 blockbuster movie, 'Ghostbusters.'

"SEE YOU LATER ALLIGATOR, AFTER WHILE CROCODILE"

Meaning

This catchphrase is used when people are parting. The colloquial, "See you later alligator" is usually responded to with, "After while crocodile."

Origin

American teens in the 1950s popularized this phrase. The song by this name was written by Bobby Charles. It was recorded by Bill Haley and His Comets and became a top 10 rock-and-roll hit!

"THROW IN THE TOWEL"

Meaning

To quit in defeat. To give up or surrender.

Origin

This comes from the boxing world when a boxer is suffering a beating and his corner wanted to stop the fight they would literally, 'throw in the towel' to indicate their conceding of the fight. The phrase 'throwing in the towel' was preceded by 'throwing in the sponge.'

"SMOOTH MOVE EX-LAX"

Meaning

Used in a sarcastic manner to describe someone's actions that are clumsy and stupid.

Origin

This phrase has been around for some time although the exact origin is unclear. It was a popular saying by teens during the 1970s in America. It refers to the laxative, Ex-Lax, that creates smooth bowel movements. Not meant in any way to be a compliment, it pretty much says to someone, 'that sure was a shitty move on your part.'

"I DON'T GIVE A RATS ASS"

Meaning

An expression of lack of concern. Meaning a person doesn't care about a particular situation in the least.

Origin

This expression comes from a whole group of idioms most likely stemming from 'not giving a damn.' Rats are often associated with negative feelings and considered worthless, especially the 'hind quarters' and was used in print in the 1953 novel, 'Battle Cry' and also in Mark Twain's 'Huckleberry Finn.'

"HOTTER THAN A TWO DOLLAR PISTOL"

Meaning

Usually used in a negative context to describe someone or a situation that is potentially bad or trouble.

Origin

This phrase is believed to have originated in reference to stolen guns that were sold cheap on the streets. Country-Western singer George Jones also referenced it in his hit, 'The Corvette Song.'

"MONEY DOESN'T GROW ON TREES"

Meaning

Meaning that money is something that must be earned and that it is not easy to acquire it. It also means you should be careful how much you spend because it isn't an infinite resource.

Origin

Although unclear exactly when or where this idiom originated, it did appear in print in 1891 in the Statesville Landmark newspaper, 'Money doesn't grow on trees here yet.'

Also, for most American kids growing up they've heard it more times than they care to remember from their parents as relating to their spending habits and the cost of goods.

"I'LL BE A MONKEY'S UNCLE"

Meaning

Used as an expression of surprise.

Origin

This comes from Darwin's 'Decent of Man', which he published in 1871 outlining his theory of evolution, sparking controversary which continues to this day. 'I'll be a monkey's uncle' originally was a sarcastic remark made by non-believers of Darwinism.

Also, during the famous Scopes trial in 1925, a Tennessee schoolteacher, John T. Scopes, was accused of breaking the law by teaching Darwin's theory of evolution rather than the biblical origins of mankind. The trial was a sensation and astonished many who had never heard that humans might be related to apes. And supposedly from this trial the expression, 'Well, I'll be a monkey's uncle', became very popular.

"RAKED OVER THE COALS"

Meaning

To reprimand someone severely. To chastise them in an angry manner, using insult and shame to hurt them emotionally.

Origin

This phrase originates in a certain torture and punishment that was done to heretics in the Middle Ages, which involved dragging the prisoner over a bed of red-hot coals.

"KNOCKING IT OUT OF THE PARK"

Meaning

"You are knocking it out of the park!" means that you are doing very well at something.

Origin

This comes from the sport of baseball and refers to when a batter hits a pitch over the outfield wall, "out of the park" and scores a home run for his team.

"THE ROAD TO HELL IS PAVED WITH GOOD INTENTIONS"

Meaning

A common meaning of this saying is that wrongdoings are often masked by good intentions, or even that good intentions, when acted upon may have unintended, negative consequences.

Origin

This is believed to have originated with Saint Bernard of Clairvaux, a French abbot and leader in the reform of Benedictine monasticism, who wrote (c.1150), 'hell is full of good wishes or desires."

"DON'T ROCK THE BOAT"

Meaning

Don't cause any disturbance, try to change anything, or mess with the current situation. To keep things just as they are so as not to upset anyone or anything.

Origin

This came from William Jennings Bryan, the American statesman, lawyer and politician, who in 1896, said, "The man who rocks the boat ought to be stoned when he gets back on shore."

"RISE AND SHINE"

Meaning

Expression used in a polite way to wake someone up. To wake up, be lively and do well.

Origin

The earliest use of this phrase in print comes from the Bible, Isaiah 60:1,. "Arise, shine, for thy light is come, and the glory of the Lord has risen upon thee.

In the 1960s, most American schoolchildren heard this from their parents every morning as they were woken up to prepare for school.

"JUMP THE GUN"

Meaning

To do something before the proper and right time.

Origin

This comes from track and field races and was preceded in the USA by the phrase "Beat the Gun." It dates back to the early 20th century when false starts were rarely penalized, the pistol generally was fired immediately after the signal "Get Set!" and unsportsmanlike runners tried to "Jump the Gun" to get a head start on the competition.

"NO HOLDS BARRED"

Meaning

This refers to someone who is no longer following any rules in their efforts to win, having no limits or restrictions.

Origin

This phrase comes from wrestling as far back as the 1800s, where certain 'holds' were sometimes barred, or illegal, depending on the style of wrestling match.

"MISERY LOVES COMPANY"

Meaning

Misery loves company means that people who are suffering are comforted, in a selfish way, by the knowledge that other people are also unhappy.

Origin

This phrase dates back to the work of Sophocles (c. 408 B.C.) the famous Greek playwright and other ancient writers. The earliest recorded use in English was about 1349.

"TWO'S COMPANY – THREE'S A CROWD"

Meaning

This usually is referring to the times when two people are alone together and don't wish to have any additional people with them, the third person becoming a 'crowd.'

Origin

The origin of this phrase is believed to be from the book, English Proverbs, in 1678. It was also translated from Spanish in 1726, so it may have origins in other ancient cultures also.

"BITE ME"

Meaning

This idiom is typically used as an expression of annoyance with someone, similar in meaning to 'Go to Hell' or 'Screw You.'

Origin

This expression originated in America in the fifties and was used in raunchy conversation referring to a specific part of their anatomy by teenage boys of that era to indicate their disapproval of actions or statements by someone.

"HOLD YOUR HORSES"

Meaning

This phrase is commonly used when telling an overly enthusiastic or anxious person to restrain themselves, slow down and be patient.

Origin

This began back in the days when travelling by horse was the norm and people were told this to control and calm an excitable horse.

It appears in the book, Iliad by Homer, which dates to around the 8th century B.C., referring to Antilochus driving like a maniac in a chariot race that Achilles initiates in the funeral games for Patroclus.

"CLOSE ENOUGH FOR GOVERNMENT WORK"

Meaning

The contemporary meaning and use of this phrase refers to a low standard of quality and poorly executed work.

Origin

This originated in World War II, meaning that when something was 'good enough for government work' it meant it could pass the most rigorous of standards. Since around 1960 it ironically has taken on a 180-degree meaning, referring to poorly executed work.

"YOU CAN'T FIX STUPID"

Meaning

Used when referring to someone who does something, well, really stupid! Dumb people, real numbskulls, generally make the same mistake over and over again, hence the reality that they aren't getting smarter and therefore 'you can't fix stupid.'

Origin

'You Can't Fix Stupid" is an album by American comedian, Ron White. Released in 2006, it peaked at number 1 on the Billboard Top Comedy Album chart.

"YOU SOUND LIKE A BROKEN RECORD"

Meaning

When someone repeats something over and over and over again in an annoying fashion, they're often referred to as 'sounding like a broken record', referring to a vinyl phonograph record that, when scratched, or 'broken', the play needle becomes stuck in the recordings groove and keeps repeating the same section over and over again until moved manually.

Origin

This expression was first used in America back around 1940.

"RUNNING IN THE RAT RACE"

Meaning

This phrase equates humans to rats and refers to the often fierce, competitive way of life that involves pursuing goals in a repetitive, endless and pointless manner.

Origin

This dates back to the 15th-century English play, 'Everyman' and was also referenced in Author John Steinbeck's 1947 novel, 'The Wayward Bus' and in song by reggae artist, Bob Marley in 1976.

"ROB PETER TO PAY PAUL"

Meaning

To take something, usually money, from one person to give back to a different person; Settling one debt by incurring another.

Origin

This comes from the Peter tax and the Paul tax in mid-16th century England and refers to times before the Reformation when Church taxes had to be paid to St. Paul's Church in London and St. Peter's Church in Rome; originally it referred to neglecting the Peter tax in order to have money to pay the Paul tax.

"SERIOUS AS A HEART ATTACK"

Meaning

Usually said to someone to let them know you're not kidding or joking around. That you're very serious.

Origin

Coming from the dangerous and potentially life-threatening medical condition of suffering a heart attack, this expression became popular in the 1960s. People would often say this in response to a statement such as 'you must be joking' in order to emphasize that they aren't joking whatsoever.

"FIGHTING TOOTH AND NAIL"

Meaning

To make a strenuous effort and use all of one's resources. To fight furiously in whatever battle or challenge one is up against.

Origin

Originating as an ancient Latin phrase; 'toto corpore atque omnibus ungulis' which means, 'with all the body and all the nail.'

Dating back to the 1500s it comes from the idea of fighting like a wild animal, with their teeth and claws.

Author Charles Dickens famously used the phrase in David Copperfield in 1850.

"WET YOUR WHISTLE"

Meaning

Commonly used with the meaning of 'to take a drink' especially an alcoholic one.

Origin

This can be found back as early as the 14th century in the poem, 'The Reeve's Tale,' by English poet Geoffrey Chaucer. In those days a person's mouth and throat were referred to as their 'whistle,' so to wet their whistle meant drinking and quenching their thirst.

"LET IT ALL HANG OUT"

Meaning

If you 'Let It All Hang Out' you're behaving in a very informal and relaxed way, doing whatever you want to do.

Origin

"Let It All Hang Out' is a classic 1967 song by the American garage rock band, The Hombres. The song was done as a parody of Bob Dylan's 1965 release, 'Subterranean Homesick Blues.' The song peaked at number 12 on the Billboard Charts in 1967.

"DIGGING A HOLE TO CHINA"

Meaning

Used when someone is digging a hole so deep that it is (humorously) supposed to be going to go right through the Earth and come out the other side.

Origin

The earliest mention of this phrase is in 1854 when Henry David Thoreau wrote in Walden, 'As for your high towers and monuments, there was a crazy fellow in town who undertook to dig through to China, and he got so far that, as he said, he heard the Chinese pots and kettles rattle; but I think that I shall not go out of my way to admire the hole which he made.'

"NOW YOU'RE COOKING WITH GAS"

Meaning

Referring to something or someone who is functioning and performing very effectively.

Origin

This catch phrase originated in the 1930s as an advertising and marketing campaign by the natural gas industry as a push for the purchase and use of gas-powered stoves.

"IT'S PROBABLY A BLESSING IN DISGUISE"

Meaning

Something that seems bad or unlucky at first, but results in something good happening later.

Origin

This is believed to have originated in the mid-1700s. Its earliest use in print was in a 1746 work by English clergyman and writer James Hervey, titled: 'Reflections on a Flower Garden.'

"GOING TO HELL IN A HANDBASKET"

Meaning

To deteriorate quickly. To proceed on a course to disaster. A situation that is not going to end well.

Origin

'Going to hell in a handbasket' seems to be a catchy and expanded version of the phrase 'going to hell'. Sinners were portrayed in paintings and stained glass as early as 1515 being carried off to hell by the devil in handcarts. One theory for the use of 'Handbasket' was their use in the axe and guillotine method of capital punishment during the 1700s in Europe. The heads were caught in the baskets and the person presumably went straight to hell upon execution.

"I'LL BE A SON OF A GUN"

Meaning

An exclamation used in an encouraging or complimentary way. Also used to express surprise or disappointment.

Origin

This phrase originated as 'son of a military man' (that is, a gun). The British Navy used to allow women to live on naval ships. Any child born on board who had uncertain paternity would be listed in the ship's log as 'son of a gun'.

"MONKEY SEE MONKEY DO"

Meaning

To copy or mimic the behavior of someone without reason or understanding.

Origin

A popular belief is that this phrase originated from West African folklore. In the tale, a hat salesman has his entire inventory of hats stolen by monkeys, who grab them while he naps under a tree, and then climb out of his reach. Upon waking, he gestures and screams angrily at the monkeys, only to have them imitate his gesturing and screaming. Finally, he throws his own hat to the ground in frustration. The monkeys do the same, resulting in a happy ending.

"AN APPLE A DAY KEEPS THE DOCTOR AWAY"

Meaning

Long associated with a healthy diet, eating an apple a day is believed to keep one's health problems to a minimum and therefore reduce or eliminate the need for a doctor.

Origin

The first recorded use of this phrase is in the 1860s from Pembrokeshire in Wales. The original phrase was, 'eat an apple on going to bed, and you'll keep the doctor from earning his bread.'

In the 19th and early 20th century the phrase evolved to 'an apple a day, no doctor to pay' while the phrase commonly used today was first recorded in 1922.

"YOU'VE MADE YOUR BED, NOW LIE IN IT"

Meaning

Said to someone who must accept the unpleasant consequences of something they have done.

Origin

This can be traced back to about 1590 and is related to the French proverb, 'Comme on faict son lict on le treuve' (As one makes one's bed, so one finds it).

"DRINKING THE KOOL-AID"

Meaning

Referring to a person who believes in a possibly doomed or dangerous idea because of perceived potential high rewards. To blindly follow someone or ideal.

Origin

This phrase refers to followership at its worse. It was coined after cult leader Jim Jones, of The Peoples Temple, led over 900 people to commit mass suicide by drinking a grape-flavored drink laced with cyanide on November 18, 1978 in Jonestown, Guyana.

"LIKE SHOOTING FISH IN A BARREL"

Meaning

Anything that is ridiculously easy to accomplish. Almost no effort or expertise required.

Origin

Prior to the modern days of refrigeration, fish were packed and stored in large barrels. The barrels were packed to the rim full of fish. As such, any shot entering the barrel would be sure to hit at least one of them. This being the case, nothing could be easier than shooting fish in a barrel.

"PLAY IT BY EAR"

Meaning

To act spontaneously and according to the situation. Playing it by ear means you have no game plan.

Origin

This phrase comes from the musician's world. When musical compositions were played without the benefit of sheet music, they either remembered it or improvised. The musician would use his/her ear to feel out the composition and follow the musical progressions.

"NOT WORTH A RED CENT"

Meaning

Referring to something that is worthless as a 'red cent' means it has absolutely no value at all.

Origin

Originally minted in 1793, the U.S. one-cent copper coin is often referred to as 'red cent', due to its copper content and is the lowest denomination of American coin. This saying became a popular method of describing the lack of value of something or someone in the early part of the 19th century. One of the earliest printed forms of this expression was in the Columbia Democrat Newspaper in Bloomsburg, Pennsylvania in 1837 describing businessmen who weren't 'worth a red cent'.

"NO NEWS IS GOOD NEWS"

Meaning

Usually said to someone to make them feel less worried when they have not received information about someone or something, because if something bad had happened, they would have probably heard about it.

Origin

This expression may very well have originated with King James I of England, who said, 'No news is better than evil news' in the year 1616.

"LET SLEEPING DOGS LIE"

Meaning

To leave things as they are; especially, to avoid restarting or rekindling an old argument; to leave disagreements in the past.

Origin

Coming from the long-standing observation that dogs are unpredictable when they are suddenly disturbed, Geoffrey Chaucer, known as the 'Father of English literature,' was one on the first to put this notion into print, in Troilus and Criseyde, circa 1380, "It is nought good a slepyng hound to wake."

"CAN'T SEE THE FOREST FOR THE TREES"

Meaning

An expression used of someone who is too involved in the details of a problem to look at the situation as a whole.

Origin

This one has been around for a very long time. One of its earliest uses was in a 1546 collection by English writer John Heywood.

"LIKE A BAT OUT OF HELL"

Meaning

Moving recklessly fast and erratic.

Origin

Bats have long been associated with witches and the occult, and therefore thought to originate in the bowels of hell, as they fly quickly as if in panic to avoid such light as might be cast by the fires of hell.

This phrase can be traced back to the Greek playwright Aristophanes' 414 B.C. work titled 'The Birds.'

In more current times, rock musician Meat Loaf released his debut album by this name in 1977 and has been one of the best-selling albums of all time as well as popularized the use of this phrase.

"WHEN YOUR SHIP COMES IN"

Meaning

When one has made one's fortunes.

Origin

There are two widely accepted origins of this phrase.

One is that during the 19th century at busy seaports, local merchants would lend credit to the wives of sailors at sea until the day the ship returned to port. When asking for credit they promised to pay the tab 'when their ship came in.'

Another version is that for centuries people invested their money in merchant shipping. When the ship returned from its voyage you got your money back with profit. Oftentimes, the ships were lost to pirates or storms so big risks were involved. You therefore only made a profit 'when your ship came in.'

"THAT'S A BUNCH OF MALARKEY"

Meaning

Insincere or exaggerated talk. Nonsense. Bullshit.

Origin

This phrase originally found favor and popular use by Irish-Americans in the 1920's. A cartoonist of Irish descent, Thomas Aloysius Dorgan popularized the phrase.

"LED ON A WILD GOOSE CHASE"

Meaning

A futile search or pursuit of something.

Origin

This phrase is very old and appears to be one of many introduced to the language by Shakespeare in Romeo and Juliet. It refers to a form of 16th century English horse racing where riders were required to follow a lead horse at a set distance, mimicking wild geese flying in formation.

"WHEN PIGS FLY"

Meaning

Referring to something that is highly unlikely to ever happen.

Origin

Derived from a centuries-old Scottish proverb. Used in various forms since the 1600s.

American author John Steinbeck was told by his professor that he would be an author when pigs flew. When Steinbeck became a novelist, he started to print every book he wrote with the insignia "Ad astra per alas porci" (to the stars on the wings of a pig). He sometimes also added the image of a flying pig, called "pigasus".

"I'M GONNA MAKE YOU AN OFFER YOU CAN'T REFUSE"

Meaning

To make someone an offer where they really have no choice. Do as I say or suffer negative and serious consequences.

Origin

Although this saying originates in the 1934 film, 'Burn Em Up Barnes', where Jason Robards' character is suggesting making a large and tempting offer of cash meant to be taken as an offer of generosity rather than as a threat, by far the most popular use of this expression came from Marlon Brando's character, Don Vito Corleone in the 1972 film, 'The Godfather'.

"LET THE GAMES BEGIN"

Meaning

Used as a means of announcing the start of any contest or competitive undertaking.

Origin

This was the order given by the emperors in ancient Greece after the sacrifices to the gods were completed to start the Olympic Games.

"YOU ARE WHAT YOU EAT"

Meaning

The idea that the food you eat directly affects your health and well-being.

Origin

Dating all the way back to 1826, French lawyer and politician Anthelme Brillat-Savarin wrote, 'Dis-moi ce que tu manges, je te dirai ce que tu es' (Tell me what you eat and I will tell you what you are). He gained fame as an epicure and authored work on gastronomy.

"IN LIKE FLINT"

Meaning

A slang phrase meaning to have easily or quickly achieved a goal or gained access as desired.

Origin

The original expression, 'In Like Flynn' referred to Errol Flynn, the romantic Hollywood actor, who had a reputation as a hard-drinking, hell-raising ladies' man and his sexual escapades.

In more recent times the phrase changed to 'In Like Flint' which was based on a 1967 film, "In Like Flint" starring James Coburn.

"TWO WRONGS DON'T MAKE A RIGHT"

Meaning

This proverbial adage means that a second misdeed or act towards someone in response to their wrongdoing to you does not cancel the first or make it right.

Origin

This appear in the Bible. Romans 12:17-21. 'Do not repay anyone evil for evil'.

"LOOSE LIPS SINK SHIPS"

Meaning

Keep confidential information confidential, because there are consequences if you don't.

Origin

This phrase originated on propaganda posters during World War II. The phrase was created by the War Advertising Council and used on posters by the United States Office of War Information to emphasize the importance of being discreet with any information that could be used by the enemy if discovered.

"THE STRAW THAT BROKE THE CAMEL'S BACK"

Meaning

Referring to a series of unpleasant events that finally makes you feel that you cannot continue to accept a bad situation.

Origin

Originally from an Arab proverb about a camel who was loaded with straw. His load grew and grew and grew until finally one last straw provided too much and caused his back to break.

Its most influential appearance in literature was thanks to Charles Dickens in Dombey and Son, published in the 19th century, "As the last straw breaks the laden camel's back."

"THERE'S NO FREE LUNCH"

Meaning

You don't get something for nothing. Anything one receives for free will ultimately be paid for in another way.

Origin

This comes from a practice in the 19th century in the United States whereby taverns provided a free lunch to their drinkers.

"DOESN'T AMOUNT TO A HILL OF BEANS"

Meaning

The idea that beans are so common that even a hill of them isn't worth very much if anything at all. The Yiddish word for 'beans' is 'bupkes,' which has been adopted into the English language to mean 'absolutely nothing.'

Origin

The older version of the saying, 'not worth a bean,' appeared as far back as 1297, when historian Robert of Gloucester wrote it in his English chronicles.

The American saying, 'doesn't amount to a hill of beans,' began to appear around 1863; 'a hill of' was often inserted into the phrase to emphasize its meaning.

"WHEN THE SHIT HITS THE FAN"

Meaning

The point at which an already unstable situation devolves into one of utter chaos.

Origin

Alluding to the unmistakable effects of shit being thrown into an electric fan, this phrase became immensely popular with the United States Marine Corps in World War II and was used as a code for a fight or action in the South Pacific Islands of Guadalcanal and Iwo Jima.

"THAT CAME OUT OF LEFT FIELD"

Meaning

Something completely unexpected happening. A surprising and shocking event.

Origin

This is an American slang that came from baseball. It refers to a play in which the ball is thrown from the area covered by the left fielder to first base throwing the batter/runner out. The throw from left field to first base is the longest in the ballpark and is ultimately incredible and unexpected if done so before the runner gets to first base.

"HERE'S YOUR SIGN"

Meaning

When someone asks a stupid question to which another person responds sarcastically and then states, 'here's your sign.'

Origin

'Here's your Sign' is the 1996 debut comedy album of Bill Engvall. It begins with Engvall stating that stupid people should be required to wear warning signs that simply state "I'm Stupid." For example, a trucker gets his truck stuck under an overpass and the responding policeman asks, "Hey, you get your truck stuck?" The trucker answers, "No sir, I was delivering that overpass and I ran out of gas. Here's your sign."

"WHEN LIFE LOOKS LIKE EASY STREET, THERE IS DANGER AT THE DOOR"

Meaning

When all appears to be going great in life with no end in sight, beware, there will be sadness and disappointment at some point in the future.

Origin

From the classic rock band, The Grateful Dead's 1970 song, 'Uncle John's Band.' Many believe it refers to the tumultuous time of that era; the Vietnam War and the Grateful Dead's own reflective feelings about love, peace and life.

"ICING ON THE CAKE"

Meaning

Referring to something positive that enhances a situation that's already good. However, it can also be used in a sarcastic manner meaning that something bad has been added to an already bad situation.

Origin

Originally this referred to the sweet, creamy toppings called the icing, added to a cake to make it even better. It has been in use since the mid 1900s.

The first example of its use in a figurative sense comes from the Broadway play, "The Sin of Pat Muldoon" written by actor and playwright John McLiam in 1957.

"GIVE AN INCH AND THEY'LL TAKE A MILE"

Meaning

Making a small concession to someone will allow that person to take advantage of you in a much larger way.

Origin

This expression, in a slightly different form, was already a proverb in John Heywood's 1546 collection, "Give him an inch and he'll take an ell." 'Ell' was a former measure of length, about 45 inches. The use of 'mile' dates from about 1900.

"ONLY TIME WILL TELL"

Meaning

Sooner or later something will become known or be revealed. Since it is impossible to predict the future, only time will tell if something will happen or not.

Origin

This phrase dates all the way back to the early 1500s although there's no written evidence of this. Lucius Annaeus Seneca was a Roman statesman and philosopher who died in 65AD. He is quoted to have said, 'Time discovers truth'.

"A DIAMOND IN THE ROUGH"

Meaning

This refers to someone or something whose good qualities are hidden. Having exceptional qualities or potential but lacking refinement or polish.

Origin

This first appeared in print by John Fletcher in 'A Wife for a Month, 1624' – "She is very honest, and will be as hard to cut as a rough diamond."

"FALLING OFF THE WAGON"

Meaning

To be 'on the wagon' is to abstain from the consumption of alcoholic beverages. To 'fall off the wagon' is to start drinking again.

Origin

The original version of this American expression was, 'on the water wagon' or 'water cart'. During the late 19th century, water carts drawn by horses wet down dusty roads. At the height of the Prohibition crusade in the 1890s men who vowed to stop drinking would say they were thirsty indeed but would rather climb aboard the water cart to get a drink rather than break their pledges. From this sentiment came the expression 'I'm on the water cart,' I'm trying to stop drinking, which is first recorded in Alice Caldwell Rice's 'Mrs. Wiggs of the Cabbage Patch' in 1901, where consumptive Mr. Dick says it to old Mrs. Wiggs.

"IF YOU CAN'T BEAT THEM, JOIN THEM"

Meaning

It doesn't mean to surrender, but rather to use the other side's tactics.

Origin

This expression is supposedly an old political adage. "If you can't lick 'em, join 'em" wrote Quentin Reynolds in the book, 'The Wounded Don't Cry', about life in London during World War II.

"BEGGARS CAN'T BE CHOOSERS"

Meaning

Those in dire need must be content with what they get. Accept what is given to you, especially if you don't have the means to acquire it yourself.

Origin

This expression goes way back in time and was recorded by English writer John Heywood in his 'Dialogue of Proverbs of 1546'.

"GOING OUT IN A BLAZE OF GLORY"

Meaning

If you go out in a 'blaze of glory' you do something in a very dramatic and impressive fashion. Not giving up, fighting to the bitter end, even though failure is all but assured. Often referring to something that someone would do at the end of their life that would ensure fame.

Origin

A popular belief is that this comes from the American Wild West. Gunslingers and outlaws in seemingly never-ending shootouts with small town sheriffs and rivals at high noon.

Rock musician Jon Bon Jovi's solo album in 1990, 'Blaze of Glory' played off of this with heavy references to the Old West and gunslingers. It was the theme song for the 1990 Western film, 'Young Guns II'.

"LIKE A BUMP ON A LOG"

Meaning

Usually used to describe someone who is greatly inactive. This inactivity may be due to being shy, being lazy, or just being stupid.

Origin

This expression presumably compares lazy, inactive people to the similar immobility of such a protuberance (bump) on a log. It was a common phrase in the mid 1800s.

"BETWEEN THE DEVIL AND THE DEEP BLUE SEA"

Meaning

In a very difficult situation, faced with two dangerous alternatives.

Origin

No one knows for sure where this phrase originated, but it's widely believed that it is nautical in origin. The 'devil' refers to the seam on a ship's hull. This seam, needed to be watertight and required filling (caulking) occasionally. While at sea this required a sailor to be suspended over the side precariously and described as being 'between the devil and the deep blue sea.'

"THIRD TIMES A CHARM"

Meaning

The belief that the third time something is attempted is more likely to succeed than the previous two attempts. It is also used as a good luck charm – spoken just before trying something for the third time.

Origin

The first of what appears to be a precursor to this phrase is in Elizabeth Barrett Browning's 'Letters addressed to R.H. Horne, 1839' - 'The luck of the third adventure' is proverbial.

It's also listed in Alexander Hislop's 'The proverbs of Scotland' in 1862: 'The third time's lucky'.

The proverbial description from the mid 19th century suggests it dates from even earlier. The most common is that it alludes to the belief that, under English law, is that anyone who survives three attempts at hanging would be set free.

"ON YOUR LAST LEG"

Meaning

If someone or something is 'on its last leg' it is in bad condition and will soon be unable to work or function properly.

Origin

Dating back to the 16th century, this saying referred to someone who was in bad financial shape, nearing bankruptcy.

"IT'S EITHER FEAST OR FAMINE"

Meaning

A situation in which something is either always extremely abundant or in extremely short supply.

Origin

Dating back to the early 1600s this phrase originally was 'feast or fast'. Sometime in the 20th century, 'Famine' was substituted to form its use today.

"THE APPLE DOESN'T FALL FAR FROM THE TREE"

Meaning

Referring to the fact that a child often has similar characteristics and behavior as his or her parents.

Origin

Originally appearing in Germany in the early 1800s as 'the apple doesn't fall far from the stem.' It was first used in English by American philosopher Ralph Waldo Emerson in an 1839 letter. But here, Emerson used it in another sense, to describe that tug that often brings us back to our childhood home.

"GREASE THEIR PALMS"

Meaning

To pay a bribe or make an illegal payment to someone in exchange for favors or influence.

Origin

Dating from 16th century British English, this evolved from the phrase 'grease the wheels' since wheels and machinery required grease in order to turn and operate smoothly. Eventually, 'grease' moved to someone's 'palm' and metaphorically changed to money.

"HIT THE ROAD JACK"

Meaning

Usually said by someone wanting another person to leave their presence immediately and not come back. Sometimes followed by adding, 'and don't come back no more'.

Origin

This saying comes from horses 'hitting the road' with their hooves. 'Jack' was added much later to add emphasis to the phrases current meaning.

Percy Mayfield wrote the song 'Hit the Road Jack' in 1961 and Ray Charles made it famous as it went to number 1 on the Billboard Hot 100.

ABOUT THE AUTHOR

Michael Schlueter is an author and photographer living with his wife Jill on a small farm in Missouri along with a variety of pets and critters. He enjoys spending time in the great outdoors, seeing new places, and sharing laughs with family and friends.

Other books by Michael include;

"101 Quirky & Crazy Phrases & Sayings"
"That's The Fact Jack-101 Strange but True Facts"
and the coffee-table fine art photography book,
"America's Bloodiest 47 Acres-Inside the Missouri State Penitentiary"

Visit Michael and see more of his work at;

www.schlueterphoto.com
www.amazon.com/author/michaelschlueter

I hope you've enjoyed this book! If so, please take a moment to leave a review on Amazon for me. Your support is very much appreciated! Thank you!

All the Best,
Michael